Adventures in Numeracy

Aliens and Astronauts

Sally Hewitt

illustrated by Serena Feneziani

Thameside Press

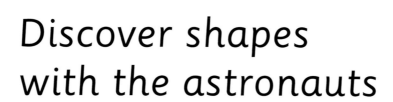

Discover shapes
with the astronauts

Countdown to blastoff! The astronauts
and their dog, Pointer, set off on a space
adventure. They touch down on Shape
World. Who will they find?

Follow the strange footprints to find
out who made them. The shape of each
footprint will give you a clue. Look for
all sorts of different shapes.

Play games with the astronauts and their
new friends, and discover that on Shape
World, shapes are everywhere!

Finally, the astronauts climb into their
rocket and zoom into space. Look for
more shapes in space.

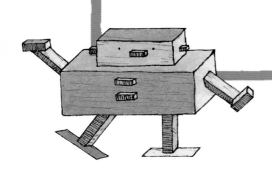

The astronauts are ready for a space adventure.

10 9 8 7 6 5 4 3 2 1 0

Press the buttons to blast off.

Get the order right!

Circle ● Rectangle ▮ Triangle ▲ Square ◼

BLAST OFF!

A sphere is round like a ball. Planets are spheres.
Point to the three biggest planets.

The rocket heads
for a strange planet.

Can you find a spaceship, a shooting star,
and a planet with two rings?

It's Shape World!
Get ready to land.

Can you find these shapes?

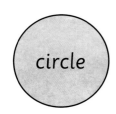

circle

What has Pointer found?

Follow the circles. Can you guess
who made these footprints?

Surprise!
The rocks turn into aliens.

sphere

The aliens are made of spheres.
Count all the spheres.

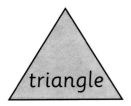

triangle

Pointer sniffs out more footprints.

Follow the triangles. Where do they lead?

These rocks are aliens too!

pyramid

The aliens are made of pyramids.
Point to the pyramids.

rectangle

Next, Pointer follows some rectangles.

Where does the trail of rectangles lead?

Suddenly the box comes to life!

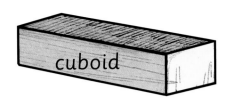

cuboid

This time the aliens are made of cuboids.
How many cuboids are there?

square

More footprints.
They're squares this time.

Follow the square footprints.
Who made them?

Alien dogs made of cubes!

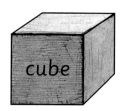

cube

Point to the cubes.

"Come with us," say the aliens.

Follow the curved path with your finger.

"We'll show you where we live."

Now follow the path of straight lines.

Welcome to Shape City!

The aliens are the same shape
as the skyscrapers they live in.

Which aliens live in each skyscraper?

The aliens take the astronauts to a palace.

More aliens line the road in a pattern:

The alien leader comes out to welcome the visitors.

Some aliens are late. Can you see who?
Where do they fit in the pattern?

"Which planet do you come from?" asks the leader.

Which shapes have curved lines, which have four corners, and which have three straight edges?

Time to play.
Spheres are good for rolling.

How many pins have been knocked down?
How many are still standing?

"Look what we can do!" laugh the aliens.

Which aliens have made themselves into an arch?

"Can you make an arch too?"

Help the astronauts copy the arch.
Do they have enough shapes?

Everyone plays hide-and-seek.

Where are the aliens hiding?
Can you tell what shape they are?

"Here we are!"

Did you guess the right shapes?

It's time to go home.
"Come back soon," say the aliens.

Which alien made each present?

"Goodbye! Thanks for a great day," shout the astronauts.

10 9 8 7 6 5 4 3 2 1 0

BLAST OFF!

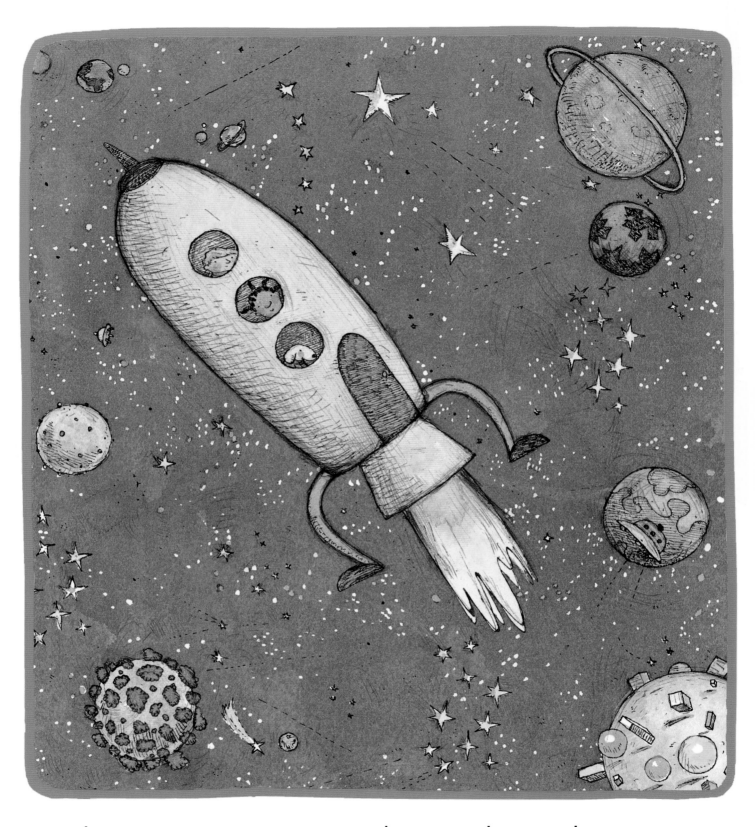

The astronauts zoom home through space.
Can you see Earth?

Notes for parents and teachers

Aliens and Astronauts will help your child to:

- Recognize 2D shapes.
- Recognize 3D shapes.
- Learn about straight lines and corners.

- Learn about curved lines.
- See how solid shapes fit together.
- See that spheres will roll.

Two young astronauts and their dog, Pointer, set off on a space adventure. They press four buttons to start their journey—a circle, a triangle, a rectangle, and a square. The aliens on Shape World are made of 3D shapes. Their footprints help you guess their shape.

Meet all the aliens on pages 8–15, then follow the curved and straight paths to find their homes.

- Circular footprints lead to aliens made of spheres.
- Triangular footprints lead to aliens made of pyramids.
- Rectangular footprints lead to aliens made of cuboids.

- Square footprints lead to aliens made of cubes.
- Follow straight and curved paths to Shape City.
- The aliens live in homes that match their own shape.

Space is full of stars, planets, galaxies, and comets. How many different shapes can you find on your space adventure with the astronauts?

Try these activities and games to help you learn about everyday shapes.

- Spot shapes everywhere you go—circular clock faces, triangular road signs, and cuboid cereal boxes.

- Cut shapes out of colored paper. Make patterns with them. Then try to fit them together.

- Make potato prints of circles, triangles, rectangles, and squares.

- Play "Name that shape." Take turns describing a shape. For example, "It has three corners and three straight sides." (A triangle.)

- Collect boxes, balls, and cardboard rolls. Stick them together to make all kinds of interesting models.

Distributed in the United States by
Smart Apple Media
1980 Lookout Drive
North Mankato, MN 56003

Text by Sally Hewitt
Illustrations by Serena Feneziani

Series editor: Mary-Jane Wilkins
Editor: Russell McLean
Designer: Jamie Asher
Educational consultants: Andrew King
    and Norma Penny

ISBN: 1-930643-55-1
Library of Congress Control Number: 2001088837

Printed in Spain

9 8 7 6 5 4 3 2 1